Inspirations *from the* Heart, Mind, *and* Spirit

P. J. JAMES-DOUGLASS

NEWMAN SPRINGS PUBLISHING
320 Broad Street
Red Bank, NJ 07701

First originally published by Newman Springs Publishing 2019

ISBN 978-1-64096-986-5 (Paperback)
ISBN 978-1-64096-987-2 (Digital)

Printed in the United States of America

In loving memory of my Mother Wilhelmina G. McPherson.

To my children, Keith, Keisha, Kip and Jewel Douglass. To my sister and brother-in-law Deborah and Timothy Williams. To my special friends, Julius Riddick, Wilma Gaines, and Earline Harris for all your support and love and for not giving up on me. Thank you for encouragement.

A special thanks to Claresa Cummings for all of your efforts and beautiful designs over the years of putting my writings into beautiful designs for special occasions. You have been there from the beginning of my writings.

Good Morning

*T*oday is a brand-new day! What are you going to do with it? The first order of the day is to be thankful that you are being able to see it. Offer up a prayer to the Heavenly Father. Ask Him what He wants you to do today. He will surely enlarge your territory if you ask Him to.

A brand-new day should bring you new thoughts and action. You might have had a project yesterday that you did not finish or could not finish because you could not see how to get it done.

Today, though, you have a better perspective of how to complete the task. Yesterday is gone and never coming back. Do not hold onto old thoughts. Give yourself the opportunity to experience new ideas, new thoughts, and new direction.

Today, start on a project that you have a passion for. It is never too late. If you have thought of going back to school, do it! If you have thought about taking a trip, do it! Whatever you had a desire to do, start putting the plans into motion.

The mornings are the best time to start planning on what you are doing to do today. Even if your day takes a different tum, and you do not get to finish what you started, do not get frustrated if you have to take a different direction. It is still a good morning.

> Lord, help me to be grateful for this morning and show me which way I should go today. Lord, help me to be a beckon of light to those around me this morning. Lord, let me speak with love not bitterness. Help me to do an act of kindness for someone today. Lord, even if I am face with

a difficult situation in my life today, help me to not dwell on it to the point where I am so focus on the problem instead of being grateful to You for this good morning. Amen.

A Ray of Hope

....

"For I know the plans I have for you," declares
the Lord, "plans to prosper you and not to harm
you, plans to give you hope and a future."
—Jeremiah 29:11–12

A Christian's hope is not based on what he sees or feels. It is based on God's faithfulness. Having hope, even just a ray of hope while we are suffering, shows we understand God's grace and mercy. Hope comes from believing God will do what He promised.

In Mark 5:36, when Jairus was going through a crisis, Jesus said, "Don't be afraid, just trust me." These are comforting words for anyone who is going through a crisis.

The words of Jesus Christ give us both *hope* and *promise*. Look at our problems from Jesus's point of view. He is the source of all hope and promise. In the midst of your worst storm, look at the situation with spiritual eyes. With a ray of hope, you will discover the solution is just over the horizon.

Are You Able to Let Go and Let God?

··

*W*hen you speak the desires of your heart, do you let them go? Love is a spiritual gift that brings forth attraction and harmony. Do you know you are to tum your thoughts to God in prayer? When you speak the desires of your heart, you activate a powerful force.

After you pray, you need to trust and believe that what you have prayed has already been taken care of. You need to let go of trying to fix the situation or solve a problem. Release any thought you may have of how your desires should manifest. God, the one source and one power, is the answer to your prayer. Spirit in wholeness when you seek health; divine love is abundance when you seek prosperity.

God is wisdom when you seek guidance. All these gifts of spirit are freely given to you as you ask from your heart.

God is love, and those who abide in love
abide in God, and God abides in them.
—1 John 4:16

Are You Allowing Peace
to Live in You?

*B*eing active and ambitious does not have to mean being frenzied and stressed. In fact, being at peace on the inside can make you much more effective on the outside. Do what you do without fighting against it. Give your presence and full attention to what you are doing while keeping your spirit in a place of peace and acceptance.

Choose your actions by being fully involved in and informed by the world around you. Choose your attitude by being ever thankful for your opportunity to experience it all. Life is constantly placing demands on you. You can choose to feel peacefully empowered by those demands and by the positive possibilities for progress that come with them.

Do not make an unnecessary burden for yourself. Instead of creating stress inside, allow peace to fill your spirit. Equip yourself in the most effective way to deal with whatever may come. Allow peace, deep inside, and act always from a place of peaceful power.

Are You Allowing Your Ability to Blossom?

*P*rogress is made by those who have the courage to be wrong and the persistence to find how to get it right. Great achievements are crafted into existence by those who, when they begin, are not sure exactly how they will do it.

Do not wait until you know how to do anything before you have the confidence to do something. Find confidence in the authenticity of your desire and the goodness of your purpose. You do not have to be an expert to gain expertise. You just have to get busy.

If you should stumble a lot at first, get back up each time and apply what you have just learned. Even when you stumble going forward, you are still moving ahead. Do not wait for confidence to come to you. Get out there and create it for yourself.

You are worthy and able to reach the goals that truly mean something to you. Get yourself going and enjoy the experience of allowing your ability to blossom.

Are You an Excuser or an Achiever?

*A*re you one who make excuses after excuses? Or are you focused on achievement? Do you live each day focus on excuses? What makes you focus on excuses? Take an inventory of self, make a list of the things you make excuses for, and ask yourself why.

Everything has a root. Find your root and pluck it up and throw it out. This will take time but put the effort toward your achievements. Find out what you are good at. You do not have to be an expert. Your interests will point you in the direction you should be focusing on.

By focusing on excuses, you would not make an attempt at things unless you get it perfect. Think about it. When you focus on achievements, you will get it done.

If you are focusing on excuses, the slightest obstacle will stop you cold. When you are focused on achievement, you will work your way through any challenge.

By focusing on excuses, you will avoid unfamiliar or uncomfortable situations. When you are focused on achievement, you will seek new, invigorating adventures and will find great value in them.

If an excuse sounds reasonable, it will satisfy you temporarily. Excuses can pull you down and cause you to miss great opportunities. Let go of the easy excuses and grab on to a burning desire for meaningful achievements.

Are You Better or Worse?

*W*hen I was thinking how to start this inspiration, I was drawn to the beginning of the year with all the New Year's hope and changes.

Let me start by saying experts give their predictions about the economy, politics, weather, and the list goes on and on. People everywhere are hoping that the year will be better than the last; no one knows what will happen.

Then I thought about what Paul said to Timothy, "In the last days, perilous times will come; evil men and impostors will grow worse and worse. But you must continue in the things which you have learned and been assured of, knowing from whom you have learned them" (2 Timothy 3:1, 13–14).

Now my spin on this topic is the inspired Word of God is to instructs, corrects, and encourages us as we follow God's path (vv. 16–17).

As the spiritual darkness of our world grows deeper, the light of Christ shines more brightly through all those who know and love Him. Jesus is our joy and hope today, tomorrow, and forever!

We must continue in the things of God even when our life is in a difficult season. To be honest with ourselves, it is hard to be positive when our lives are in a turmoil! Let's not kid ourselves. A bad report from our spouse, doctor, children, supervisor, family, or friend can turn our lives upside down.

The answer to the question "Are we better or worse?" is not easy. During those times of uncertainty, we *must* draw on His Word on a daily basis. We have to be consistent with our affirmation. If we want to make life better, we *must* speak, mediate, and keep junk from entering our spirit.

A song, message, passage, and conversation can turn on the lightbulb for you. In those moments, the spirit is guiding you. Remember, we are always *better*.

> Heavenly Father, the trouble in this world can divert our eyes from You. Thank You for Your Word that helps us stay focused. May we find our delight in Your love and share it with others today.

The power of the evil around you is no match for the power of Jesus within you.

Are You Capturing Every Thought?

....

*B*e careful what and who you allow into your mind because your thoughts rule your life. Fact, you get thoughts every day from various sources: at home, at work, being with family and friends, and even during your quiet time. Thoughts are with you every day, every moment. You might wonder how can you manage your thoughts successfully. Here is one way that might help. You can transform your thoughts by making a decision to submit our thoughts to Jesus. "All authority in heaven and on earth has been given to you."

Remember Jesus controls everything in heaven and on earth. He has the final say about everything, including your thoughts. Jesus has more authority than your parents.

People—including parents, teachers, counselors, and others—may treat you with injustice, call you worthless, but Jesus says you are valuable. He has the authority over everything, even you. When unpleasant things happen to you by the hands of others who are supposed to guide and train you, it can leave an everlasting effect on you.

Submitting your mind over to Jesus is not easy. You have to be committed to the Word, get yourself some index cards or notepad, and write scriptures down to draw on when you are having a pitty-pat moment. In time, your thoughts will not be focused on the hurt and disappointments (see 2 Corinthians 10:5, Matthew 28:18).

Are You Doing What Is Right?

I do not know about you, but sometimes, I find it hard to do what is right. For example, when someone deliberately does or says negative remarks or acts toward me or someone else, it is hard for me to keep my mouth and attitude intact.

What keeps me in check (sometimes), I know that my action would not be Christlike. And yet I sometimes get in the flesh and speak out. Then I feel real bad about my actions. I then have to say, "Keep on scrubbing, Lord."

I think all people are supposed to be kind, caring, loving, and patient toward others; it is not easy all the time. Sometimes you will have to hold your peace to keep the peace. It took me a long time to *learn* this principle and *apply* it. I still have to pull in my reigns at times. I have not arrive totally.

Now let me get to the meat of the topic, do not settle for what is convenient or popular. We must do what is right regardless of how we feel or think. It can make all the difference to someone and/or to ourselves.

Do what is right for yourself merely because this is your life, so honor yourself and fulfill the wonderful potential that lies within. When you do what is right, you will not have any regrets! We can set the stage for life even when it is difficult, even when the flesh is at war with the spirit.

Are You Enjoying Your Life?

*E*njoy your life on this day in this place, whatever concerns, challenges, opportunities, and situations you are faced with. Enjoy yourself. Enjoy the little seemingly insignificant things. Enjoy the big life-altering things.

Enjoy the drama and the peace, the solitude and the fellowship, and the activity and the relaxation. Enjoy the work and the play. Enjoy being you. Enjoy not having to impress anyone just being able to live your life in harmony with your values.

You work better, play better, sleep better, eat better, and experience better relationships when you allow yourself to enjoy.

It is really not that difficult to make the choice to enjoy your life. Enjoy your life in an authentic way and make it a whole lot more enjoyable.

If you are not enjoying your life, it is about time that you start. All of us have trials, tribulations, heartaches, disappointments, illness, and uncertainty. Life goes on, so why not you. Make the most of whatever state you are in. *Enjoy, enjoy, and enjoy you!*

Are You Experiencing Abundant Blessings?

A re your eyes open to the unlimited blessings of God?
God's blessings multiply when we open our eyes to them. We see and experience the blessings of God every day. Some of our blessings are subtle, as when we bump into a friend we have not seen in a long time or find a perfect gift. Other blessings are more significant, a promotion, celebrate birth of a child, or marriage.

God's blessings are always within and around us. Our part is to be open to them, to be aware of the activity of God at work in our lives, and maintain an attitude of gratitude.

Through our increase awareness of God's blessings, we find happiness in the little things and joy in the big things.

Thank You, God, for abundant blessings. Scripture reading: Psalm 144:15.

Are You Following Your Own Advice?

···

*I*f you knew someone in your own situation, what advice would you give to that person? What course of action, what priorities, what strategies would you suggest?

Think about that, and then think about this. Are you right now following your own advice?

It is easy to know what to do when you are not the person who has to do it. When you actually have to implement the advice, things can get complicated and uncomfortable.

Yet good advice is good advice. And you are well-positioned to give yourself good advice.

Yes, it will involve some real work to do what you know must be done. Fortunately, as difficult as it may be, you can absolutely do that work and follow the advice you yourself would offer.

So go ahead, be brutally honest and give yourself the advice you need to hear. Then take it to heart, put it into action, and make the progress you know you can make.

Are You Grateful for the Lessons in Your Life?

....

*A*s you watch the children head back to school, have you reflected on how much you are still learning? Do you look for lessons in your actions, reactions, and feelings? Do you turn within on challenging days? Do you listen to your inner wisdom and learn how you may have handled a situation better next time?

Do you give thanks for everything you have learned from finding a shortcut, saving you time to discerning when to make your next big move?

Every encounter is a chance to learn. It would be worth seeing with eyes of curiosity, wondering what insight you may gain from each interaction. Release judgment and replace it with acceptance and gratitude. When there are patterns you want to change or reinforce, open yourself to spirit guidance.

God shows you the next right action. Lifelong learning leaves you fulfilled and at peace.

Are You in a Storm?

G etting on board with Jesus does not mean you will never go through a storm. Jesus said, "In the world, you will have tribulation" (John 16:33, NKJV). In spite of God's promise to protect and prosper us, you will still have to deal with things like disease, lack, and fear. The difference is the unbeliever faces the storm without Christ, but as a believer, you go through the storm confident that all will be well because Jesus is onboard. Does this mean you will never experience panic or fear? If only this was true, but it is not! It's in Matthew 8: 23–24 and Mark 4:38.

Fear can be deadly, it corrodes your confidence in God's goodness. It unleashes a swam of doubts. It deadens your spirit. Fear creates a form of spiritual amnesia. It dulls your miracle memory. It makes you forget what Jesus has done and how good God is. That is why you must starve your doubts and feed your faith on God's Word. Faith is what will take you through the storm.

Are You in the Need of Healing?

You are healthy in mind, body, and spirit. You may need healing in your body, finance, marriage, job, or household. If so, you are not feeling your best. Remember wholeness is the divine blueprint for your mind, body, and spirit. Use your power of imagination to envision perfect health.

With that vision in mind turn within to bless and thank each part of your situation, knowing every cell of your being seeks to express the wholeness of God.

When you feel confused or adrift, recall your constant connection with Spirit. Then come back to the wholeness of God. Release any mental, emotional, or physical resistance to complete healing. As you remain focused on wholeness, say out loud I am healed in mind, body, and spirit. I am at ease as I move and breathe.

The healing power of spirit is always present. Remind yourself that every time an adverse situation shows itself.

On the day I called, you answered me,
you increased my strength of soul.
—Psalm 138:3

Are You Okay with What You Cannot Change?

*T*here are people who do not understand you. *Be okay* with that, and then work in a positive way to encourage more understanding. There are things that will happen to set you back. *Be okay* with that and be ready to quickly recover from the disappointments.

Life is not always fair. *Be okay* with that, find the beauty anyway, and do all you can to offer genuine compassion to those who suffer from unfairness.

This day may not turn out exactly the way you planned. *Be okay* with that and make use of it anyway. You may not like what has already happened, but there's nothing you can do to change the past. Your best strategy is to let it be what it has been, *be okay* with it, and move toward the future you wish to create.

Invest your time and energy in new positive efforts where they will make a difference, not in bitterness about circumstances from the past. *Be okay* with the way things are and be in a position to make them much better.

In Every Detail

Whatever you are doing, put your passion, love, full attention, and awareness into it. Give all you have to even the smallest of acts.

The richness of life is created in the living of it. Fulfillment comes not from getting, taking, having, or keeping but from being and becoming.

In every detail of your life, there is the opportunity for greatness. The more of yourself you put into all you do, the more successful you will be.

Real life starts now; it is not a trial period. Find what your passion is and focus on it with a strong commitment to see it through.

Give your energy, your attention, your thoughts, and your love to what you are doing right now. Put yourself fully into what you do, and whatever you do will be of much value.

Remember, there is no task too small or too large to ignore. Make life rich by living every moment, giving of yourself, think greatness, and then get busy doing; every act will give you great fulfillment.

Are You Pure in Heart?

....

G od is forever active in our life and in the lives of others. In Acts 17:28 in God, "We live and move and have our being." Yet sometimes we fail to remember the Christ is with us in all situation. Daily drama or current events may cause us to feel separated from Spirit. We may forget our true nature.

We have the power to overcome feelings of separation. It would be nice that in our daily prayer, we tum our attention to the healing power of God. As we pray, a cleansing should occur. Thoughts of fear and preparation should be released. The truth of love and oneness should fill our minds and free our hearts. With clarity restored, we will see God and good everywhere. We are pure in heart, and we are blessed.

> Blessed are the pure in heart,
> for they will see God.
> —Matthew 5:8

Are You Skillful?

I have a mind filled with wisdom and a heart filled with love. I may have made mistakes because I lacked the knowledge or skill to handle a certain situation. Yet feeling guilty is pointless and only hurts my self-confidence. Instead, I see where I have made mistakes, take responsibility for them, make amends, and let them go. I trust I am becoming more skillful in my interactions and relationships.

As an expression of Christ, I am innately wise and loving. I see myself acting skillfully in difficult situations, listening to my mind and heart. I approach every circumstance with peace and understanding.

Guided by Spirit, I express patience, acceptance, forgiveness, and grace. I behold the Christ in myself and in others. I am wise, loving, and grateful.

This may be a difficult task to accomplish at times. There are people who are very negative and have nothing good to say about nothing or no one. And yet they may be in your circle of acquaintances. This is where your skillfulness really comes into action.

> For wisdom will come into your heart, and
> knowledge will be pleasant to your soul.
> —Proverbs 2:10

Are You Troubled by
Trivial Inconveniences?

···

*T*he vast majority of what you consider problems, when viewed in a historical context, are nothing more than trivial inconveniences. That's because a whole lot of people who came before you made the choice to leave life better than they found it.

By the standards of that same historical context, if you are not improving life, you are not living fully. No matter where you are or what you have, you always have the opportunity to move life positively forward.

You have the capacity to be creative, productive, and effective. To the extent you utilize that capacity, you experience life's richness.

Those problems and those trivial inconveniences do not have to slow you down for more than a short while. You are far more powerful than any problem that might come along.

In fact, the challenges give you all sorts of ways to utilize your capabilities and to create new value. Get out there, meet those challenges head-on, and discover how you can connect to the best life has to offer.

Step back from the day-to-day distractions and consider all the great things you can do. Then step forward and find great satisfaction in making your world a more enriching and fulfilling place.

Exercise Your Heart

*T*o exercise your heart, get rid of hatred, unforgiveness, malice, and the like. Replace it with compassion, love, forgiveness, and joy. Once you get rid of the baggage stored in your heart, it will function better. Your attitude, mood, and outlook on life and yourself will be brighter.

When you hold on to hurtful issues, it eats at your attitude, mood, and heart. The choice is up to you. It is good to guard your heart, but when you exercise your heart, it is a sweet aroma that fills the air.

Have you been around someone, and they are genuinely happy, a big smile, a pleasant attitude all the time? And you know that this person has lack in their life, has been hurt, disappointed, lied on, and mistreated but seems to have such a sweet aroma about them. You have seen them crying and broken.

Their attitude leaves you in disbelief. Because you knew them when... Over time, they learned not only to guard their heart, but also they learned to exercise their heart. They are truly a testimony for all of those whose heart needs exercising.

Give Yourself

Who are you giving yourself to? Are you giving yourself to your job, friends, family, spouse, or children? We get so wrapped up in these things until we have to squeeze time for prayer, reflection, his promises, and going to church. And when we do, we are tweeting, thinking about what we have to do and places we have to go.

The Lord wants us to give ourselves to Him. He wants to have a relationship with you and bring you to a new and higher spiritual level where you can begin to see things in a new perspective. By doing so, your life will unfold new opportunities to prepare you for the way you should go. He wants you to trust Him.

Put all the unnecessary junk out of your life and get to knowing your Father by giving yourself to Him. Let Him take you from level to level and from glory to glory. So when those difficult situations arise in your life, you will not fall apart. You will have the strength to say to your mountains, "My Father is bigger than you." Have substances that you can draw on His Word, His promises, and His reflections.

> Lord, help me to stay grounded in you in the midst of trials and tribulations. Help me to put aside all that is not of You so that I can focus on You to worship, to have a prayer life, not just when I am in trouble. Lord, I want to have a relationship with You.
>
> Lord, help me to open my spiritual eyes, ears, and heart so that I can hear You, see the direction I am to take, and open my heart to understand what You want me to do. Amen.

Guard Your Heart

....

*C*ircumstances can be a reason for you to lose heart. It is easy for you to want to give up and give in. Your emotions can run amuck in you. At this time, you talk to anyone who will listen. This may not be the best thing to do, but your emotions are running high.

Your circumstances can and will cause you to leave your heart wide open for negativity. Know who you are talking to. This can be an important part of your solution. Be selective of whom you open up to. Not everyone has your best interest at heart.

Step back, regroup your emotions and thoughts, take time to calm yourself. By doing so, you will get a clearer revelation as to how to get to a solution. Always take your concerns to the Lord; He will guide you in the right direction. Sometimes the Lord will lead you to a person who will speak just want you need to hear and the direction you need to take!

In times of uncertainty, your heart is the most vulnerable. Remember, guard your heart.

I Miss You

....

I remember yesterday when I took time for granted.
I thought I can do it later. I know they would not mind.
But here it is, tomorrow. Time has gone too quickly.
I need to tell them what is on my mind.
I want to thank them for being mine; always there beside me.
Even through the toughest times, their wisdom guided me.
And when they disagreed with me, they were usually right.
Yet they never turned away, they just reminded me, "I am here for
you." On those many lonely nights, my *best* friend, they would be.
My love one was there, without a doubt, to
love and reassure me that I was loved.
I miss your smile. I miss the holding of hands.
I miss your laughter. I miss the warm touch.
I miss your walk. I miss that special look.
I miss you knowing what I was thinking before saying a word.
I miss how you would comfort me after a long day. I miss our talks.
There are not enough words to express what you
meant to me, nor how much *I miss you*!

Now Be Thankful

*B*e thankful for the discomfort. It pushes you to move yourself forward.

Be thankful for the dissatisfaction. It reminds you, and it compels you to make more positive choices.

Be thankful for the frustration. It helps you to discover more effective ways of taking action.

Whatever the world throws in our path, be thankful for the opportunity to experience it. Be thankful in a state of sincere gratitude to discover the treasure that has just been laid at your feet.

There is never any good reason to feel sorry for yourself and never any good result to come of it. There is always a way to be thankful.

Touch the beauty, grasp the richness, live the wonder suddenly available in this moment to you.

Step Beyond the Limitations

....

*D*o not take refuge in seeing yourself as a victim. Take pride in getting yourself to do good and valuable things. Everybody has problems and limitations and extenuating circumstances. Yet progress is always possible no matter what. Sure, there is unfairness, and there is injustice in the world. Work to right those wrongs but do not fall into the trap of using them as excuses.

When you choose to move forward, there are all kinds of things that could go wrong. But that is no reason to hide from life or to remain stuck where you are. You do not have to be defined by your disappointments, injuries, or limitations. Choose instead to define yourself by your highest visions, dreams, goals, and ambitions.

You are a unique, creative bundle of positive possibilities, so live your life that way! There is so much good you can do, so let go of the excuses, step beyond the limitations, and make more of the goodness happen today.

The Power of Your Faith

*I*n times of difficulties, challenges, and confusion, do you give in to your doubts and fears? The fact is that we all get to a moment where we doubt our faith or better yet do not use our faith.

When we speak with authority about a situation, we build up our faith to take the next step. Our words have power; therefore, our faith has power. Why are we not using our faith power to get solutions to our circumstances?

Fear will and can cause you to question your faith when you cannot see a quick solution to a situation. One of the best ways to put your power of faith at work is to never stop praising and worshipping God in and at all times.

Use the Power

Y ou have the power to make your life better. Use it. You have the power to transform difficult situations into valuable achievements. You have the power to successfully work through whatever challenges lie in front of you.

If you are stuck in an unsatisfying rut, you have the power to get unstuck. When circumstances change, you have the power to adapt and to prosper. It does not matter that you have abused or neglected your power in the past. What matter is that you can use your power now.

You have the power to choose your thoughts and to choose your actions. You have the power to focus your time, your energy, and your life in a positive, rich, and meaningful direction. You have the power to fill your world with the best things you can imagine. Imagine those beautiful things without limit and use your power to make them so.

About the Author

My inspiration for this book came out of my own life experiences, struggles, and uncertainties. Through prayer and meditation, my desires became clearer as to what I wanted out of life, and that is to be the best- version- of myself in everything I encountered.

I had to learn that the past is just that the past. Once I realized this important fact my mind and heart was open for new beginnings. I cherish, nurture, appreciate and love what I have more deeply.

CPSIA information can be obtained
at www.ICGtesting.com
Printed in the USA
LVHW092329210719
624814LV00001B/72/P

9 781640 969865